Animal Spikes and Spines

Rebecca Rissman

www.raintreepublishers.co.uk
Visit our website to find out
more information about
Raintree books.

To order:
☎ Phone 0845 6044371
🖹 Fax +44 (0) 1865 312263
🖥 Email myorders@raintreepublishers.co.uk

Customers from outside the UK please telephone +44 1865 312262

Raintree is an imprint of Capstone Global Library Limited, a
company incorporated in England and Wales having its registered
office at 7 Pilgrim Street, London, EC4V 6LB – Registered company
number: 6695582

Edited by Daniel Nunn, Rebecca Rissman, and Harriet Milles
Designed by Joanna Hinton-Malivoire
Picture research by Tracy Cummins
Originated by Capstone Global Library Ltd.
Production by Victoria Fitzgerald
Printed and bound in China by Leo Paper Products Ltd

ISBN 978 1 406 22901 1 (hardback)
15 14 13 12 11
10 9 8 7 6 5 4 3 2 1

British Library Cataloguing in Publication Data
Rissman, Rebecca.
   Spiky and spiny. – (Acorn plus)
   1. Animal defenses–Pictorial works–Juvenile literature.
   2. Spines (Zoology)–Pictorial works–Juvenile
   literature.
   I. Title II. Series
   591.4'77-dc22
A full catalogue record for this book is available from the British
Library.

Acknowledgements
We would like to thank the following for permission to reproduce
photographs: iStockphoto **pp. 7** (© Brandon Alms), **9** (© Ken
Canning), **15** (© Craig Dingle), **21 left** (© Tom Tietz), **21 right**
(© beltsazar); Minden **p. 17** (© Donald M. Jones); National
Geographic Stock **p. 20 right** (© PAUL NICKLEN); Shutterstock
pp. 4 (© Utekhina Anna), **5 left** (© Hiroshi Sato), **5 right** (© irin-k),
10, **22c** (© Ronnie Howard), **11**, **22a** (© Nick Biemans), **12** (©
ecoventurestravel), **13** (© Maria Dryfhout), **14** (© FloridaStock),
16, **22f** (© MartinMaritz), **18**, **22d** (© Hazeelin Hassan), **19**, **22e** (©
Francois Etienne du Plessis), **20 left** (© Undersea Discoveries), **22b**
(© Four Oaks).

Cover photographs reproduced with permission of iStockphoto (©
Grafissimo and © Paul Tessier), Photolibrary, and Shutterstock (©H.
Damke and © Kate Connes). Back cover photo reproduced with
permission of Shutterstock (© MartinMaritz).

We would like to thank Michael Bright for his invaluable help in the
preparation of this book.

Contents

Some words appear in bold, **like this**. You can find out what they mean in "Words to know" on page 23.

Animal body parts

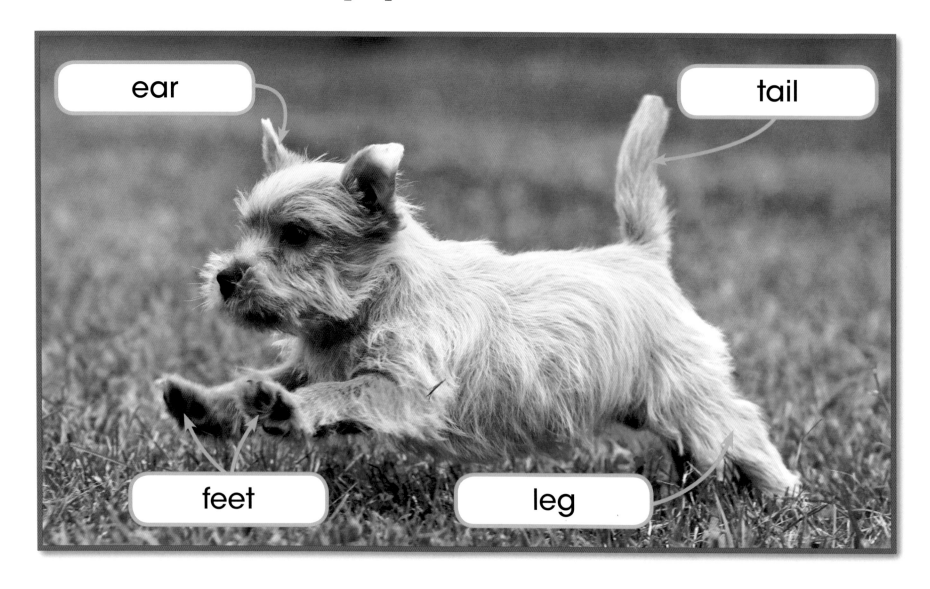

ear

tail

feet

leg

Animals have different body parts. Some body parts help animals get around. Body parts such as legs and feet help animals run. Body parts such as flippers and fins help animals to swim.

fin

flipper

eye

ear

nose

mouth

Some body parts help animals **sense** the world.
Animals use their eyes to see. Animals use their
ears to hear. Animals use their noses to smell.
Animals use their mouths to taste.

Why do animals have different body parts?

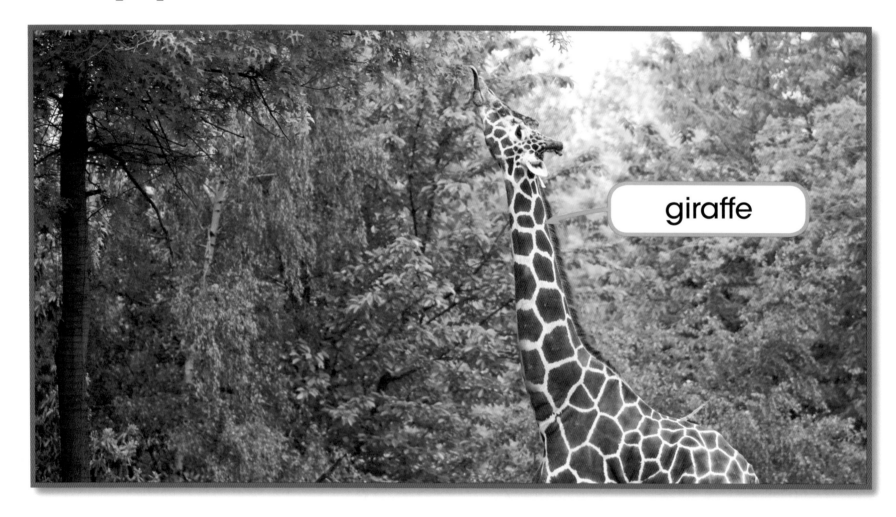

giraffe

Animals have different body parts to help them to survive. Animals live in different **habitats**. Animals have body parts that help them to live in their habitat.

frog

Some animals are **predators**, or hunters. Their body parts help them to catch **prey** to eat. Some animals are prey. Other animals hunt them. Their body parts help them to stay safe.

Ready to fight

antelope

horns

Some body parts help animals to fight. Some animals use **horns** to fight. Horns grow from animals' heads. Antelope use their horns to fight other antelope.

heron

beak

Some animals use **beaks** to fight. Beaks grow on birds'
heads. Beaks can be sharp. Beaks can be strong.
Herons uses their beaks to peck at other herons and
other animals.

antlers

moose

Some animals use **antlers** to fight. Antlers grow from animals' heads. Antlers are very hard. Moose sometimes use their antlers to fight other moose to see who is stronger.

tiger

claws

Some animals use **claws** to fight. Claws grow on animals' feet. Claws can be very sharp. Tigers use their claws to fight other tigers and other animals.

Ready to hunt

cayman

teeth

Some body parts help animals hunt. Animals hunt in order to catch and eat other animals. Some animals' teeth can be very sharp. Cayman catch **prey** with their sharp teeth.

snake

fangs

venom

Some animals' teeth are very long. Some snakes have long teeth called **fangs**. They use their fangs to catch prey. They bite other animals and put **venom** into their bodies. Then they eat them!

eagle

talons

Some animals use **claws** to catch **prey**. Claws can be very long. Eagles have long claws called **talons**. Eagles use their talons to snatch animals off the ground. They can snatch fish out of water, too.

beak

pelican

Some animals use **beaks** to catch prey. Beaks can be very long. Beaks can be very wide. Pelicans can use their beaks to catch fish. They scoop up the fish in their big beaks.

Ready to scare

spines

porcupine

Some body parts help scare other animals away.
Some animals use **spines** to scare other animals
away. Spines can be long. Porcupines use their
spines to scare other animals away.

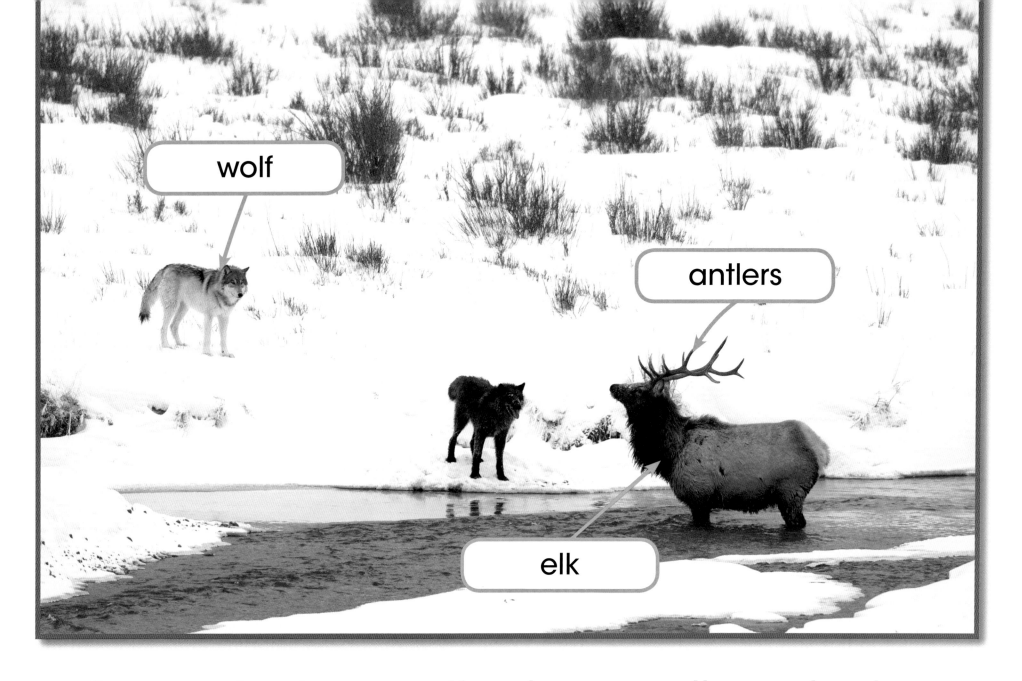

wolf

antlers

elk

Some animals use **antlers** to scare other animals away. Elk use their antlers to scare away **predators**, such as wolves.

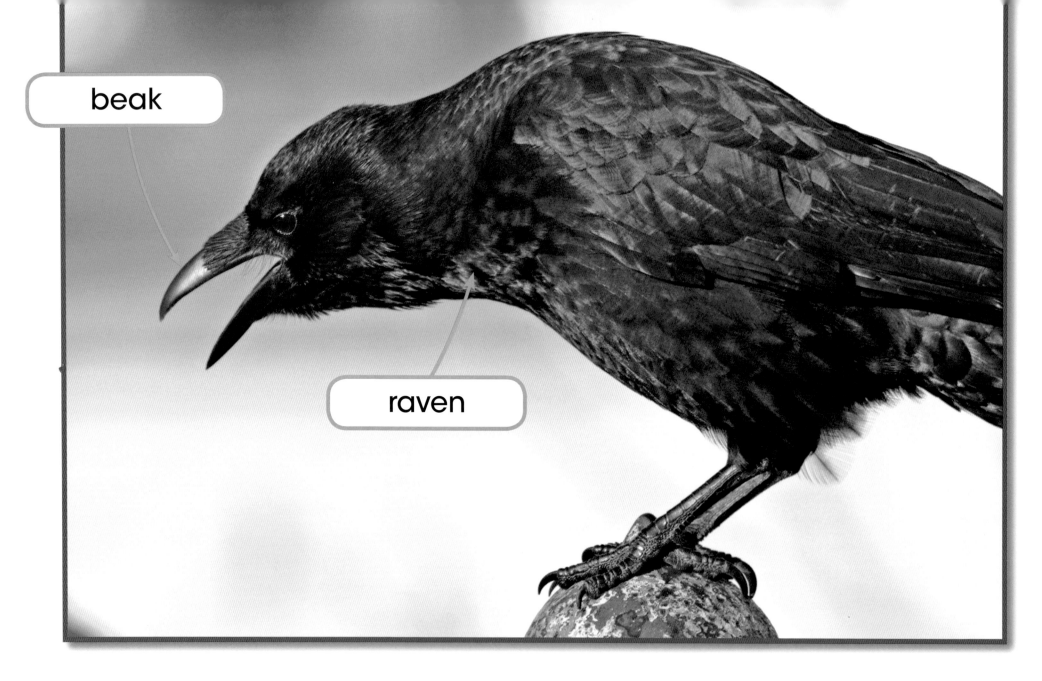

beak

raven

Some birds use sounds to scare away other animals.
This raven opens its **beak** to let out a loud warning.
It tells other birds and animals to stay away.

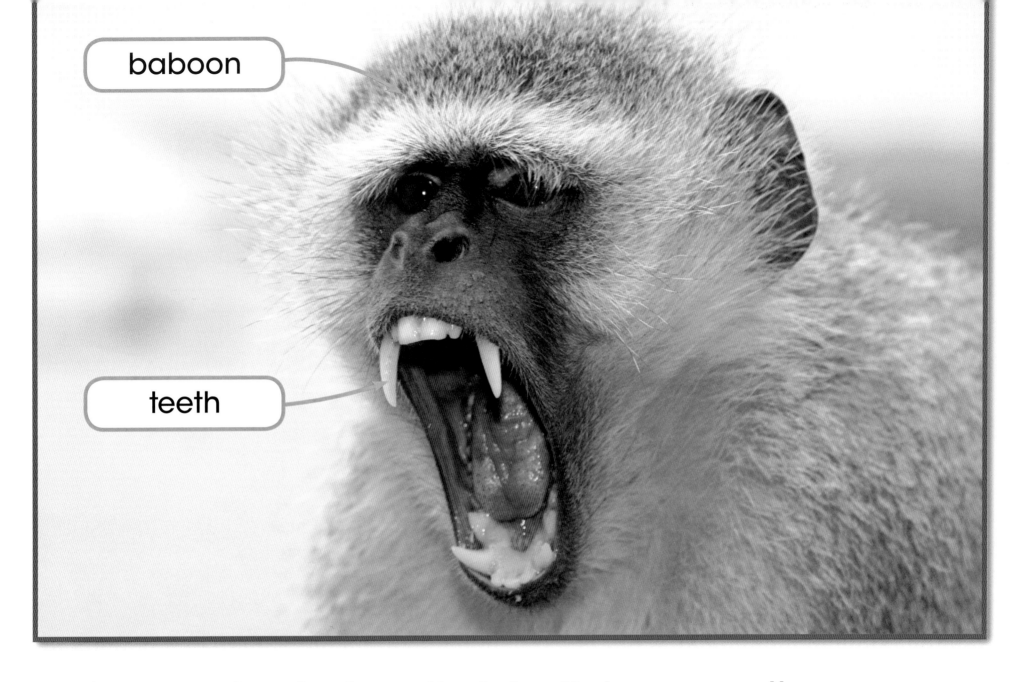

baboon

teeth

Some animals show their teeth to scare other animals away. This baboon shows its long, sharp teeth to warn other animals to stay away.

Finding spikes and spines

sea urchin

spines

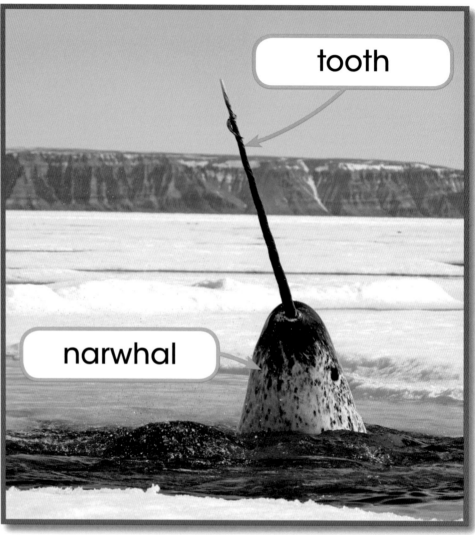

tooth

narwhal

Animals all over Earth have spikes and **spines**. Sea urchins live in the ocean. They use spines to keep fish away. Narwhals live in the ocean near the North Pole. They use a long tooth to fight other narwhals.

horn

lizard

parrot

beak

Horned lizards live in the desert. They use their **horns** to scare other animals away. Parrots live in forests. They can use their **beaks** to fight with other birds.

Animal body parts close up

a

b

c

d

e

f

Can you remember what all these animal body parts are called?

Answers on page 24

Words to know

antler hard body part that grows on the head of an animal, such as a moose

beak hard, pointed part of a bird's mouth

claw long, pointed nails that grow on some animals' paws or feet

fang long, sharp tooth of a fierce animal

habitat place where an animal lives, or a plant grows

horn hard, pointed object that grows out of some animals' heads

predator animal that hunts and eats other animals

prey animal that is hunted and eaten by other animals

sense ways that animals understand the world around them. Seeing, smelling, tasting, hearing, and feeling are senses.

spine stiff spike that grows on some animals, such as porcupines

talon long, hooked claw on the foot of a large bird

venom poison that some snakes produce to kill their prey

Index

Answers to quiz on page 22:
a) claws b) horns c) antlers d) beak e) teeth f) spines

Notes for parents and teachers

Before reading

Show the children the front cover of the book. Guide children in a discussion about what they think the book will be about. Tell children that animals have different body parts that are used for different things.

After reading

- Pass around some pictures of animals with different body parts. Tell the children to go back to their seats with a partner and sort their animals into different body part groups. For example, animals with sharp teeth, animals with tails, and animals with spikes. Then ask the children about particular animals. For instance: "Does a tiger have a beak?" (No); "Does an antelope have horns?" (Yes).